Your life can be
   what you want it to be...
You'll make it through
   whatever comes along.

Within you are so many answers.
   Understand, have courage,
      be strong.

Douglas Pagels

Other books in the *"Language of"* Series...

Blue Mountain Arts®

☆ ☆

The Language of

COURAGE
and
INNER STRENGTH

A Blue Mountain Arts® Collection

Edited by Douglas Pagels

Blue Mountain Press ®

SPS Studios, Inc., Boulder, Colorado

Library of Congress Catalog Card Number: 99-18692
ISBN: 0-88396-508-9

ACKNOWLEDGMENTS appear on page 48.

Certain trademarks are used under license.

Manufactured in Thailand
Fourth Printing: April 2000

This book is printed on recycled paper.

Library of Congress Cataloging-in-Publication Data

The language of courage & inner strength : a collection / edited by
   Douglas Pagels.
      p.   cm.
    ISBN 0-88396-508-9 (alk. paper)
      1. Courage--Literary collections.   I. Pagels, Douglas.   II. Title: Language
   of courage and inner strength.
   PN6071.C815L36   1999
   179.6--dc21   99-18692
                                                                      CIP

SPS Studios, Inc.
P.O. Box 4549, Boulder, Colorado 80306

Contents

(Authors listed in order of first appearance)

Turn to the Courage
Within You

It takes a strong person to deal with tough times and difficult choices. But you are a strong person. It takes courage. But you possess the inner courage to see you through. It takes being an active participant in your life. But you are in the driver's seat, and you can determine the direction you want tomorrow to go in.

Hang in there... and take care to see that you don't lose sight of the one thing that is constant, beautiful, and true: Everything will be fine — and it will turn out that way because of the special kind of person you are.

So... beginning today and lasting a lifetime through — hang in there, and don't be afraid to feel like the morning sun is shining... just for you.

Douglas Pagels

If you can walk,
you can dance.
If you can talk,
you can sing.

☆ Zimbabwe Proverb

We never know how high we are
Till we are called to rise
And then if we are true to plan
Our statures touch the skies.

☆ Emily Dickinson

You gain strength, courage and confidence by every experience in which you really stop to look fear in the face. You are able to say to yourself, "I have lived through this... I can take the next thing that comes along."

You must do the thing you think you cannot do.

☆ Eleanor Roosevelt

There are times in every life
when we feel hurt or alone...
But I believe that these times
when we feel lost
and all around us seems
           to be falling apart
   are really bridges of growth.
We struggle and try to recapture
      the security of what was,
      but almost in spite of ourselves...
we emerge on the other side
with a new understanding,
         a new awareness,
         a new strength.
It is almost as though
      we must go through the pain
         and the struggle
            in order to grow
and reach new heights.

 Sue Mitchell

Courage comes and goes.
Hold on for the next supply.

Thomas Merton

During trying times, keep trying!

Anonymous

Be of good courage.

Psalm 31:24 (NKJV)

Although the world is full of suffering,
it is also full of the overcoming of it.

⭐ Helen Keller

Out of suffering have emerged
the strongest souls.

⭐ E. H. Chapin

Learn what it means, "When I am weak, then
I am strong." Gather confidence thus…. No lack
in the universe but there is a supply. The deeper
the pit, the readier are the waters to fill it.

⭐ Amos R. Wells

I am not bound to win, but I am bound to be true. I am not bound to succeed, but I am bound to live up to the light I have.

☆ Abraham Lincoln

We have enough light given to us to guide our own steps.

☆ George Eliot

When you have no choice,
mobilize the spirit of courage.

 Jewish Proverb

Fall seven times; stand up eight.

 Japanese Proverb

What would life be if we had
no courage to attempt anything?

 Vincent van Gogh

It is the greatest of all mistakes to do
nothing because you can only do a little.
Do what you can.

Sydney Smith

Take courage, and turn your troubles…
into material for spiritual progress.

☆ St. Francis de Sales

A wise man once said, "Whatever came
to me, I looked on as God's gift for some
special purpose. If it was a difficulty, I
knew He gave it to me to struggle with, to
strengthen my mind and my faith." That
idea has sweetened and helped me all of
my life.

☆ Anonymous

The answer to prayer is slow;
the force of prayer is cumulative.
Not until life is over is the whole
answer given and the whole
strength understood.

☆ Stopford Brooke

Practice in life whatever you pray for, and God
will give it to you more abundantly.

☆ E. B. Pusey

To every difficult duty...
is a charm, known only
to those who have the
courage to undertake it.

 Madame Swetchine

Do your duty in all things.
You cannot do more. You
should never wish to do less.

 Robert E. Lee

I'd like to do everything I can to avoid being an old person who says, "Why didn't I do that? Why didn't I take that chance?"

Barbra Streisand

We need the courage
to start and continue
what we should do,
and courage to stop
what we shouldn't do.

☆ Richard L. Evans

All mankind is divided into three classes. Those that are immovable, those that are movable, and those that move.

☆ Arabian Proverb

We cannot make the sunshine, but we can move away from that which may cast a shadow on us.

☆ Rev. C. H. Spurgeon

Courage conquers all things.

> Ovid

Raise your sail one foot and you get ten feet of wind.

> Chinese Proverb

Be not anxious about tomorrow. Do today's duty, fight today's battle, and do not weaken and distrust yourself by looking forward to things which you cannot see and could not understand if you saw them.

Charles Kingsley

Courage Is...

...the thing.
All goes if courage goes.

Sir James M. Barrie

...the foundation of victory.

Plutarch

...like love; it must have
hope for nourishment.

Napoleon

...like a kite; a contrary wind raises it higher.

J. Petit-Senn

...doing what you're afraid to do.

 Eddie Rickenbacker

...considered as an essential
of high character.

James A. Froude

...the generosity of the highest order, for the
brave are prodigal of the most precious things.

C. C. Colton

Oh courage... oh yes! If only one had that.

Henrik Ibsen

There are many… who can meet terrible danger… without shrinking, who count themselves but very timid folk, and never dream of the strong courage that is packed away under their quiet frames.

☆ Phillips Brooks

People are like tea bags.
You find out how strong they are
when you put them in hot water.

☆ Anonymous

It is in men, as in soils, where
sometimes there is a vein of
gold which the owner knows
not of.

☆ Jonathan Swift

Have courage for the great sorrows of life, and patience for the small ones; and then when you have accomplished your daily task, go to sleep in peace. God is awake.

 Victor Hugo

Courage begun with deliberate constancy, and continued without change, doth seldom fail.

Appias

We never have more than we can bear. The present hour we are always able to endure. As is our day, so is our strength. If the trials of many years were gathered into one, they would overwhelm us... but all is so wisely measured to our strength that the bruised reed is never broken.

 H. E. Manning

When you encounter difficulties and contradictions, do not try to break them, but bend them with gentleness and time.

St. Francis de Sales

Whenever two ways lie before us, one of which is easy and the other hard, one of which requires no exertion while the other calls for resolution and endurance, happy are those who choose the mountain path and scorn the thought of resting in the valley. These are the men and women who are destined in the end to conquer and succeed.

☆ Anonymous

Do not pray for easy lives. Pray to be stronger men. Do not pray for tasks equal to your powers. Pray for powers equal to your tasks! Then the doing of your work shall be no miracle, but you shall be the miracle.

☆ Phillips Brooks

Do we know that more than half our trouble is borrowed?... Just suppose that we could be sure of final victory in every conflict, and final emergence out of every shadow into brighter days; how our hearts would be lightened, how much more bravely we should work and fight and march forward!

This is the courage to which we are entitled.

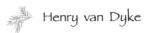 Henry van Dyke

Be strong and of good courage;
do not be afraid, nor be dismayed.

 Joshua 1:9 (NKJV)

We are never without help.
We have no right to say of
any good work, it is too hard
for me to do, or of any sorrow,
it is too hard for me to bear.

Elizabeth Charles

We work in the dark —
we do what we can —
we give what we have.

☆ Henry James

Be willing to have it so. Acceptance of what
has happened is the first step to overcoming
the consequences of any misfortune.

☆ William James

Victory is won, not in miles but in inches. Win a little now, hold your ground, and later win a little more.

Louis L'Amour

God does not take away trials or carry us over them, but strengthens us *through* them.

E. B. Pusey

There is nothing on earth
    a man need fear,
Nothing so dark or dire;
Though the world is wide,
You have more inside,
You can fight fire with fire!

> Charlotte Perkins Gilman

There is always the battle to be fought
before the victory is won.

> Dean Stanley

What counts is not necessarily
the size of the dog in the fight —
it's the size of the fight in the dog.

Dwight D. Eisenhower

Never give up and never give in.

Hubert H. Humphrey

By asking for the impossible,
obtain the best possible.

☆ Italian Proverb

If we attend… to the little
that we can do, we shall ere
long be surprised to find
how little remains that we
cannot do.

☆ Samuel Butler

The fact is, that to do anything in this world worth doing, we must not stand back shivering and thinking of the cold and danger, but jump in and scramble through as well as we can.

☆ Sydney Smith

A man of courage is also full of faith.

☆ Cicero

Courage consists not in blindly overlooking danger, but in seeing it and conquering it.

Jean Paul Richter

What on earth would a man do with himself if something didn't stand in the way?

H. G. Wells

All actual heroes are essential men,
And all men possible heroes.

 Elizabeth Barrett Browning

We can all be heroes
in our virtues,
in our homes,
in our lives.

James Ellis

Life only demands from you
the strength you possess.

⭐ Dag Hammarskjold

If we are strong, our character will
speak for itself.

⭐ John F. Kennedy

Courage and exertion —
these seem to be the
weapons with which we
must fight life's long battle.

☆ Charlotte Brontë

You must try to get along
the best you can.

 Walt Whitman

Come... let us take courage,
and hand in hand pursue our
journey in the path of life.

 Thomas A' Kempis

Your presence is a present to the world.
You're unique and one of a kind.
Your life can be what you want it to be.
Take the days just one at a time.

Don't put limits on yourself.
So many dreams are waiting to be realized.
Decisions are too important to leave to chance.
Reach for your peak, your goal, your prize.

Nothing wastes more energy than worrying.
The longer one carries a problem,
   the heavier it gets.
Don't take things too seriously.
Live a life of serenity, not a life of regrets.

Count your blessings, not your troubles.
You'll make it through whatever comes along.
Within you are so many answers.
Understand, have courage, be strong.

 Douglas Pagels

ACKNOWLEDGMENTS

We gratefully acknowledge the permission granted by the following authors, publishers, and authors' representatives to reprint poems or excerpts from their publications.

Westminster John Knox Press for "You gain strength..." from YOU LEARN BY LIVING by Eleanor Roosevelt. Copyright © 1960 by Eleanor Roosevelt. All rights reserved. Reprinted by permission.

Warner Books, Inc. for "We become more..." from SIMPLE ABUNDANCE by Sarah Ban Breathnach. Copyright © 1995 by Sarah Ban Breathnach. All rights reserved. Reprinted by permission.

Meredith Corporation for "I'd like to..." by Barbra Streisand from LADIES' HOME JOURNAL. Copyright © 1988 by Meredith Corporation. All rights reserved. Used with the permission of LADIES' HOME JOURNAL.

Hazelden Publishing and Education for "We need the..." by Richard L. Evans from NIGHT LIGHT by Amy E. Dean. Copyright © 1986, 1992 by Hazelden Foundation. For "Victory is won..." by Louis L'Amour from TOUCHSTONES: A BOOK OF DAILY MEDITATIONS FOR MEN. Copyright © 1986, 1991 by Hazelden Foundation, Center City, MN. All rights reserved. Reprinted by permission.

Alfred A. Knopf, a subsidiary of Random House, Inc., and Faber & Faber, Ltd. for "Life only demands..." from MARKINGS by Dag Hammerskjold, translated by Leif Sjoberg and W. H. Auden. Copyright © 1964 by Alfred A. Knopf, Inc. and Faber & Faber, Ltd. All rights reserved. Reprinted by permission.

Random House, Inc. for "What on earth..." by H. G. Wells from QUOTABLE BUSINESS by Louis E. Boone. Copyright © 1992 by Louis E. Boone. All rights reserved. Reprinted by permission.

A careful effort has been made to trace the ownership of poems and excerpts used in this anthology in order to obtain permission to reprint copyrighted materials and give proper credit to the copyright owners. If any error or omission has occurred, it is completely inadvertent, and we would like to make corrections in future editions provided that written notification is made to the publisher.

SPS STUDIOS, INC., P.O. Box 4549, Boulder, Colorado 80306

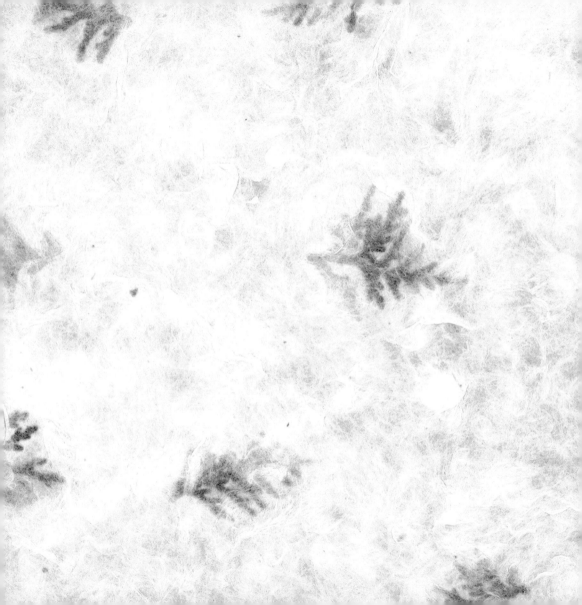